Bishop Harry,

What an honor to have met you! We love God connections. It's so refreshing hearing your powerful teaching on legacy.

In Him,
Bryan + Rhonda Matthews

P R A Y E R
A HOLY OCCUPATION

WWW. visit nlcc. com

new Life Church

Bryan Matthews cell
706 840-4003

pastor bryan @ visit nlcc.com

PRAYER
A HOLY OCCUPATION

BY
RHONDA MATTHEWS

HOUSE OF PRAYER
PUBLISHING

House of Prayer Publishing
Evans, GA 30809

Visit our website at houseofprayerpublishing.com

Printed in the United States of America

Second Edition: March 2013

ISBN-13: 978-1-4826-7590-0

CONTENTS

INTRODUCTION

What qualifies me to write a book on prayer? In Mark 11:24 it says, "Therefore I say to you, whatever things you ask when you PRAY, believe that you receive them, and you will have them. 25 And when you stand PRAYING, if you have anything against anyone, forgive him that your Father may also forgive you your trespasses. 26 But if you do not forgive, neither will your Father in Heaven forgive your trespasses."

I want to include the Message Translation of those same verses. "That's why I urge you to PRAY for absolutely everything, ranging from small to large. Include everything as you embrace this God-life, and you'll get God's everything. And when you assume the position of PRAYER, remember that it's not all asking. If you have anything against someone, forgive only then will your Heavenly Father be inclined to also wipe your slate clean of sins."

Have you ever heard the saying, "They were born with a silver spoon in their mouth?" I was born to a mama who taught me the most powerful principle: always walk in love and forgiveness. My mama wasn't hypocritical. It wasn't "do as I say, not as I do." She has always lived this love walk. It's because of this that I believe I've been able to be an effective PRAY-ER.

Mama is my biggest fan; she calls me Angel. She has always told me that I wasn't a pain in childbirth and I've never caused her any pain. Mama is also very optimistic. Remember I said that she always walks in love and forgiveness? I'm so grateful that she forgave me of something I did when I was 12 years old.

Mama was a rural mail carrier and I remember her coming home one afternoon after delivering the mail and telling me that she was listening to a preacher on the radio while on her route. She said this preacher, Kenneth Copeland, was teaching on the baptism of the Holy Ghost and the importance of a prayer language. My mama believed she needed what he was teaching so she asked for her prayer language right there in her mail vehicle! She told me she heard "shala-ma-keta". In case you are wondering what word is that, it was other tongues! "What Mama? We don't believe in that!" Can you picture this? Here I was a 12 year old telling her mom what we did and did not believe in. At 23 years old I had to call Mama and tell her not only did I believe in that now, but I had been filled with the Holy Spirit and had my prayer language. The Apostle Paul wrote in 1 Corinthians 14:15 (NKJV), "I will pray with the spirit, and I will also pray with the understanding."

I pray that you will take your assignment on the earth very serious and realize first and foremost you are here for Him. He needs you to "Occupy until He comes," and that "Prayer is a Holy Occupation." I pray these pages inspire you and encourage you to become "A House of Prayer."

Pastor Rhonda Matthews

CHAPTER 1
A Holy Occupation

Prayer a Holy Occupation, those words have resonated in my spirit for years. I know it's time to write this book with the title: Prayer a Holy Occupation.

Bryan and I both grew up in Godly homes. We both asked Jesus into our hearts at a very young age. As far as growing in the faith goes that did not happen until we were baptized in the Holy Spirit.

The story that you are reading is one of faith and faithfulness. The Word says the Holy Spirit will be your teacher. I pray before you put this book down that you will have fallen so in love with the person of the Holy Spirit and that you realize He has an assignment just for you. When you cooperate with Him, life will be so exciting and fulfilling!

I walked the church aisle of Hopeful Baptist Church on Easter Sunday when I was 6 years old and asked Jesus to be my Savior. Our family's pastor was Ron Drawdy and we were very close to him and his wife, Joyce. He and his family moved away to pastor in another city. I think the fact that he was my pastor when I asked Jesus in my heart made such an impact on me. I always said, "When I grow up and get married, will you please come back to Augusta, Georgia and perform my wedding?" He said he would. Little did I realize at that time the Holy Spirit was orchestrating that desire.

Bryan and I married on August 29, 1981. Ron Drawdy kept his word and came from Florida to marry us.

I don't know how many young couples decide at the end of their honeymoon to go to church but for Bryan and me it was a great decision. We stopped back in Jacksonville and spent the night with the Drawdys and went to church with them. It was a Baptist church but something was so different at this church. They had drums and a guitar in the sanctuary! We had never seen such things. People were clapping, and some were even dancing! When Pastor Ron began to preach, it was so enjoyable, so alive! Bryan and I joked that his preaching was better than a movie! We did not know at the time that he and his family were filled with the Holy Spirit. We just knew that the Word was alive when he preached.

Several years passed and we continued to attend church but knew something was missing in our relationship with God. Bryan and I had been married a few years now but personal growth was not happening. I personally had a desire to read His Word but honestly did not feel I comprehended what I was reading. I have such a wonderful mama who had a passion for teens and when she taught I understood. Growing up we had nightly family devotions. One of my brothers played the piano and the rest of us enjoyed singing. We had our God time and it was always so special. But now I was searching for more.

Thank God for divine agitation. One day at a Sunday service, I looked at my watch at 11:50 am and thought in 10 minutes we will be out and on our way to the lake. The boat was already hooked up to the truck and I had done my Christian duty by coming to church first. Imagine that! As Bryan and I were walking across the church parking lot, I remember looking up and saying, "God I know you created us for more. I just don't know how to get to know you more."

I don't recall how I knew that Pastor Ron had started a church in Jacksonville that was called a "Christian Center". One day in a most innocent prayer, I asked God to lead me to a "Christian Center." Should I be surprised that God loves to answer prayer? In the Saturday newspaper was an advertisement for a new church meeting in the YMCA that was a "Christian Center." Bryan would be working day shift on this Sunday morning so I called a friend and asked her if she would be interested in trying this church with me the next day. She said of course, so we went to church and arrived a few minutes before 11. Both my mama and my husband were very conscious of being on time, so according to my Baptist church hour, I was a little early. I walked into the service and it was already going. They were about to receive the tithes and offerings. I thought this was a little strange that they had no music but when the pastor got up to speak the word, it didn't matter to me that there had not been any music, wow! The Word was alive like when Pastor Ron had spoken back in 1981. I was so excited and could hardly wait to tell Bryan that I thought I had finally found the church we'd been looking for! Because of Bryan's work schedule and some traveling we were doing, it would be several weeks before he could attend with me. It had been about my 4th time arriving just before 11 that God had a supernatural set up for me. A lady named Linda Dunaway walked up to me after church was over, put her arm around me, and said, "Little friend, why do you come to church at 11?" I said, "What time does church start?" You would think I would not have been so clueless after weeks of coming to church and never hearing any music, just offering and message. I include this in my story because I know there may be people reading this that would have been like me. Our tradition did not include people lifting up their hands and sometimes we have a little trouble adjusting to change! As desperate as I was for my relationship with God to grow, He knew how to ease me into the things of the Spirit!

The time finally worked out so that Bryan could attend service with me. We were going to a Sunday night service and on our way to the YMCA, Bryan said to me, "Now this is not a church that they are going to draw attention to us and make us say our name is it?" I said, "Well of course not." I had been four times and never had any attention drawn to me as a visitor. Guess what happened that night? The pastor said, "We have a couple of visitors, how about you two stand up and say your names and the rest of the church go shake their hands and introduce yourselves!" Oh no! I could not really believe this was happening. My husband is a quiet unassuming man who does not like any attention drawn to him. He said to me later that this was the first time pride may have been used for good because he was too prideful to just walk out of the service. He thought to himself, I don't care how good Rhonda says this man can preach, I'm never coming back! Bryan also said this was his first spiritual vision. He said he had HUGE WALLS up and had no intention of receiving anything from the message that night. I love the Holy Spirit; He was able to break down every wall my husband had put up! You need to understand my husband was so shy that he did not even say the blessing in front of me for the first five years of our marriage. Now an entire church had come by to shake our hands and he had to say his name in front of them all. Well Bryan survived the initial shock and told me on our way home that he had made up his mind that this preacher wasn't getting in, but God had other plans. That preacher got in.

CHAPTER 2

Beginnings in the Spirit

Bryan and I began to attend this church. He worked shift work and came when he was off work. Our pastor, Mark Wallace, was speaking on Mark 16: 15-20 when we began attending. We were familiar with Matthew's account of the Great Commission, but this pastor taught things we had not seen before: things like casting out demons, speaking with new tongues, laying hands on the sick and they will recover. Why had we never seen these scriptures in our Bible? We were both excited about the Word; we were hungry for all He had for us. We were both baptized in the Holy Spirit on the same day.

My story is quite humorous and I can hardly believe as I write this that I really did this. Brother Kenneth Hagin had mini books on Why Tongues? and The Bible Way to Receive the Baptism of the Holy Spirit. I studied these books, looked up the scriptures, and told Bryan that I was going to receive the Baptism of the Holy Ghost. I was convinced this power was for everyone. Bryan went to work on an evening shift, and I was so excited about what I was going to ask God for that night. I had heard people talk about having a prayer closet. I didn't have one, but maybe my clothes closet would work? I scooted dresses out of the way and climbed into my closet. It was not a walk in closet. I put my hands up in the air and said, "Lord, I see this is in the Word and I want to be filled with the Spirit with the evidence of speaking in other tongues." No sooner had those words come out of my mouth, I said, "Ugh, Lord! I think I've changed my mind! What if I can't wear lip stick? What if Bryan and I don't have this great marriage anymore because I may become weird if I speak in tongues and he doesn't!" I made my way out of that closet so sad and disappointed with myself.

I knew the Baptism of Holy Spirit was for all who desired so why had I changed my mind? Bryan got home at about 12:15 and he saw I was not myself. I had a horrible headache and we both, even though we had not yet spoke in tongues, knew that Mark 16:18 said, "lay hands on the sick and they shall recover." Bryan laid hands on my head and prayed in Jesus name for the pain to go! Anytime we had any physical attacks we prayed in Jesus name and it left. This time it wasn't working! What was happening? I went to bed that night with so many questions and woke up the next morning to a pounding headache. The phone rang and a very Godly woman said to me, "The Lord shows me you have a headache." I said, "Yes. Can you pray for me?" She said to me, "That pain is because you've worked yourself up over speaking in tongues and it's not going to leave until you are filled with the Holy Spirit." All I could think was how am I going to be filled with His Spirit? My prayer closet thing did not work! I don't know why I had this desire but I wanted God to baptize me in the Holy Spirit without anyone laying hands on me.

Sunday morning came and I had invited some family to go to church with us. We were in the worship service and my head was still hurting. We were singing "El Shaddai" when the pastor had a word of knowledge and said over the microphone, "Someone has asked God Himself to baptize you with the Holy Spirit and if that person will just lift your hands toward Heaven, you will be filled." Wow, God cared about the prayer I had prayed and spoke a word of knowledge just for me! I slipped my hands up and rivers of living water began to flow out of my inner most being. I was speaking in a language I had never been taught by man. I might add that I was not wearing water proof mascara and when the Holy Spirit so marvelously filled me, I wept and black ran all down my face. This all happened during the worship service. I cleaned up my face the best I could and got ready to hear the Word preached.

Pastor Mark had an altar call for salvation and also if anyone wanted to be filled with the Holy Spirit to put their hands up. I had my eyes closed and had no idea that Bryan had put his hand up to be filled with the Holy Spirit. Suddenly I can't believe what I'm hearing. I hear the pastor say, "Bryan I see you lifted your hand to be filled with the Holy Spirit, why don't you come on down?" What! He's calling my shy husband out by name, this is not gonna be good! I was wrong Bryan was eager to be filled with the Holy Spirit and we both were baptized in the Holy Ghost on that same November Sunday morning! I left church speaking in tongues and headache gone!

CHAPTER 3

Growing in the Holy Spirit

We were both so excited that we had our prayer language and both began to be real students of the Word. We were hungry for all that was available in Him. Naturally when you taste and see that the Lord is good, you want to give back to Him. Bryan became an usher. I was thrilled to be an usher's wife and serve on the altar with tissues and prayer cloths. We both volunteered to set up church for Sunday services on Saturday night at the "YMCA". One of the visions of the pastor was to have home cell groups. We both felt to go to one that wasn't closest to our home. Romans 8:14 (NKJV) says, "For as many as are led by the Spirit of God, these are sons of God".

We began to drive each week to Linda Dunaway's for Home Group. After a few weeks of going to her home, she would lay hands on us to answer the call of God on our lives. Call of God on our lives? We only knew of two callings, a pastor and a missionary to Africa, neither of those appealed to our flesh! Little did we know then how God would put both pastoring and Africa in our hearts. Never say never!

We continued to grow and volunteered in areas needed in the church. I began to teach the 4 and 5 year old Sunday class. We became youth leaders and our pastor noticed this calling on our life too. He asked us if we'd be interested in opening our home for a home cell group. We prayed about it and felt it was part of God's plan. There is no greater joy for a Christian than to use the gifts He has placed in our lives. As I was becoming a student of the Word, I saw 1 Corinthians 14:1 (NKJV) "Pursue love and desire spiritual gifts, but especially that you may prophesy". I rather innocently began to pray that God would use me in the gifts of the spirit and that I would desire to prophesy. Looking back, the Holy Spirit had to have unctioned me to pray that prayer, that was not a natural desire. Although today I lead worship and preach the word, the thought of even holding a microphone then was frightening. I began to make it part of my daily prayer life that He would use me in the gifts of the spirit. Apparently I was not expecting Him to take my prayer for this serious!

I will never forget that first Sunday morning when the Holy Spirit was moving. I felt His presence on me so strong that I did not know what else to do but get on my knees right where I was at, on my row beside my husband. The pastor said, "Someone has been praying for God to use you in the gifts of the spirit and He desires to use you." What? Not yet Lord, I'm just not ready. Bryan gently nudges me and says, "I think the Holy Spirit wants to use you." I looked up and said, "I know, but I'm not ready!!"

When I left church that day I really could not believe that I had prayed to be used and yet I did not yield when He moved on me. I immediately repented and asked God to not use me in the gifts of the spirit because I am sure He could see I was not ready. I was certain that He would honor this prayer.

The very next week after spending the afternoon with friends we were on our way to Sunday night service, my face started tingling and I said to my friend Julie, "My face is tingling but it's not the Lord." She said, "Why did you say that?" Then I tell everyone in the vehicle, "Let's all say I will not disobey the Holy Spirit." Worship service was amazing and I was really enjoying His presence when I began to get that unction again that I had the week before. Oh No! I prayed God please don't use me this way. Why is He moving on me again so soon? Then the pastor who was very prophetic said, "The Holy Spirit desires to use someone. He moved on that person last week and they did not obey."

What! Did God show him it was me last week? I had so many crazy emotions going on in me. Do I run out of church or do I stay? Then the pastor said to look at the person next to you and say, "I will not disobey the Holy Spirit." My friend Missy McElmurray looked at me and said, "Don't you dare say that because you are who He is trying to use." Thoughts of am I going to be struck dead right here and now in this service ran through my head. The next thing I remember, I was running to the front of the church and saying, "Pastor it's me but I'm afraid!" He laid hands on me and I was slain in the spirit. As I was laying thereon the floor, I heard very clear in my spirit, "Rhonda, if you don't yield tonight, the devil will shut your voice down." I tried to negotiate with the Lord and I told Him, "But I only heard two words Lord, if you would give me a few more then I will yield." He spoke back to me that if I didn't trust Him with the two words then I would have trouble trusting in the future. Ouch! I wanted so badly to obey but this was all so different than my traditional church. I decided that I would trust and speak the two words I heard. As I tried to sit up and speak the power of His Spirit knocked me back down. I was aware the ushers stepped over me as they took up the tithes and offerings. Finally I felt I could get up off the floor.

By now the pastor was in the middle of his message. I managed to get to the front row and I literally shook under the tangible presence of God. The thought of the enemy shutting my voice down if I didn't yield tonight was overwhelming to say the least. It did not look like there would be an opportunity to even obey. At the end of the service, the pastor invited people to join the church and then the entire church was in a big circle holding hands singing, "Bind us together Lord bind us together." How was I going to obey God? There did not look like there would be a place for this little girl who had prayed to be used in the gifts to be used. Had I been so disobedient that He would not be able to ever use me? Suddenly as I was thinking these thoughts the pastor said, "Earlier tonight the Lord was moving on someone to prophesy. If that person would come and release that word now." What? Release a word? So with my very together self I stepped forward and said, "Well, I only heard two words but here goes…" I was so thrilled to hear Pastor Mark say that that was God! Whew! I've had many people ask me what I prophesied that night and I truly do not remember. I left that service begging God to not use me to prophesy again anytime soon. Couldn't He see I wasn't ready?

CHAPTER 4
Youth Callings

It was so exciting to open our home to have a home group as we continued to grow in the Lord. When we opened our home, other more seasoned teachers came to teach our group. Then came the day that our pastor thought we were ready to teach by ourselves. We were given an outline to use. Although I may be the more outgoing personality of the two of us, I was perfectly content to let Bryan do the teaching and I could be hospitality. Bryan worked shift work and the time came that he would not be able to teach at the home group one week. He and the pastor felt I should be ready! I, on the other hand, felt otherwise. Didn't they know that I was the one who had trouble getting out a prophecy just a few weeks earlier?

I decided I would attempt to teach the group. I studied the outline, but my how fear struck me. It just did not seem I could do this. We had a leadership meeting scheduled over the weekend and I will never forget sitting in that meeting where a lady from Tulsa, Oklahoma, Linda Turner, was speaking. She was sharing about her love and calling for teens and I could feel an excitement in my spirit that I may have a similar calling. While I'm sitting there thinking about what she's saying, she turns and points to me to stand up in the aisle and says, "You gift of teaching, come out of her!" The power of God literally picked me up and threw me on that little concrete chapel floor. I heard people go, "oh my" as if they hoped I didn't get hurt. Then I heard Pastor Mark say as I was laying on the floor, "If that was God she won't be hurt, if it wasn't she should not have fallen out." Well it was all God, I got up off that floor unharmed and literally the fear that had tried to grip me over teaching was gone! I felt free! The Word says in Proverbs 25:11 NKJV, "A word fitly spoken is like apples of gold in settings of silver." This word of knowledge released at the right time set a course for my life that has forever shaped my destiny.

I pray that as you're reading these pages that something inside of you will begin to desire the gifts of the spirit to excel in the Body of Christ. Linda Turner, that I had never seen before this night, went on to say over me that a similar assignment she had for teens was also on my life. It wasn't very long before that word would begin to be fulfilled. Bryan and I had served as youth leaders and the youth pastors were going to be stepping down. Our pastors came to us and asked if we were willing to become the youth pastors. We had no training for ministry. Bryan had gone to school for electro-mechanical engineering and I had gone for fashion merchandising. So how did this qualify us to be youth pastors? We accepted the volunteer position and found ourselves right in the center of the will of God! We were passionately in love with young people and committed to see them grow into their God potential. As I write this, many of the young people in that very first youth group back in the late 80's are a part of our lives and ministry today. You never know who and what your "YES" to God may affect.

One of those young people was a long haired young man that said he came to church not for salvation but "galvation". If you have ever been a part of youth ministry, you know that pretty girls and handsome fellows seem to help grow youth groups. Amy Dunaway was the bait to bring in this young man, Phillip Maxwell. Bryan and I had the privilege of leading him to the Lord at 18 years of age. Today, Phillip and Amy Maxwell are a huge part of our lives and the four of us together started the ministry where Bryan and I are senior pastors. They serve as the most awesome gifts anyone could ever ask for. They are amazing associate pastors. (I will share more of the launching of JAM Ministries in another chapter.)

With no formal Bible training just a love for God's word and a realization that the Holy Spirit is present in us today to teach and pray through us, we set out to become the youth pastors to these young people.

Of course every successful youth ministry will have fun activities. As we were enjoying this new volunteer assignment, I heard these words in my spirit, "If you play with them, you can also pray with them." So I took that very serious and invited the youth group to come out to our home on Friday nights for a time of prayer. This was truly the most fulfilling thing we had done yet in the Lord. To see young people opt to come and pray on a Friday night versus a football game or go to parties with friends was amazing! It was these Friday night prayer meetings that birthed inside of me my passion for prayer. I was eager to find young people who had my same passion to pray and participate with the Holy Spirit in prayer. The first young person that I noticed that had a passion for His presence was Amy Dunaway. Oh how she loved the Lord! I would put a demand on that anointing I saw inside of her and many of those Friday nights I would have her lay hands and prophesy over her peers. I don't really remember how many years we had these prayer meetings but I do know that only God can sustain and cause young people to opt for a prayer meeting over hanging out with peers who weren't doing the spiritual thing. We realize many of the things we are walking in today were prayed out all those years ago by a hungry group of young people.

CHAPTER 5

Prophetic Words

On April 18, 1988, our pastor took us to a prophetic conference. We knew in the Word that in Ephesians 4:11-12 (NKJV) it says, "11And He Himself gave some to be apostles, some prophets, some evangelists, and some pastors and teachers, 12for the equipping of the saints for the work of ministry, for the edifying of the body of Christ."

We had seen the ministry of pastors, teachers and evangelists but this was our first experience of the ministry of the prophet. We were there with our pastors and other leaders from our church enjoying the preaching of the Word when one of the prophets looked at Bryan and I and called us to come up front. This was our first prophetic word and much of what was spoken over us that night has come to pass today. I will share some parts of that first prophetic word here. Over me it was spoken that He would make me a worship leader in the house of the Lord. Me, a worship leader in the house of the Lord! I can carry a tune but absolutely have no musical training; I can't even read music. Who would want me to lead worship? No sooner had those thoughts crossed my mind that I heard the prophet speak over Bryan, "I am giving you the heart of a shepherd. But first, I am going to cause thee to work with young people. Be faithful in this for I will make thee a pastor says the Lord. You will teach them My Word and instruct them in My Word." Oh, I get it God, my husband will be the one who has me lead worship in the church he pastors! Seriously that seemed to be as unlikely as anything I'd ever heard, yet we were faithful to have the entire prophetic word transcribed. The Word tells us to wage a warfare with the prophecies spoken over our lives. That is found in 1 Timothy 1:18 NKJV.

I remember our pastor calling us in for a meeting the next week asking us if we intended to start a church. He said he knew those prophets to be accurate. Can I tell you that the will of God is so very important in all of our lives, but when you mess up His timing it's as though you've missed the will of God. I thank God for the person of the Holy Spirit who bore witness in our spirit that it was certainly not the timing of God to start a church. We told our pastor that we were totally fulfilled in youth ministry and did not see young people as a stepping stone to becoming senior pastors.

On a side note let me say that it would not have been God for us to start a church at that time. God is a God of order and His timing is always perfect. We must be willing to wait on Him to open doors that no man can shut, and shut doors no man can open, according to Revelation 3:7. Then we will find ourselves in the perfect will of God.

Even though it resonated in our spirits that this was an accurate word, God allowed us to be tested and see if we would wait on His timing. We knew that the timing was not right to start a church. We had the largest home group in the church. We were the youth pastors and were very involved in many other areas of the church. God is not the author of confusion and to have started a church at that time would have affected too many lives in an adverse way.

Sometime later we started a drama team that traveled in and around our area called Fishers of Men. It soon became evident that we could no longer be the youth pastors, have the traveling drama team and still give our best to the youth group. We turned in our resignation and we put our full attention into the young people who had such a hunger to do great things for God. We made a promise to the Lord that before we ministered anywhere in drama that we would take the time to pray as a drama team for the people God had us minister to. This one habit of pre-praying before a service has been the reason we've had success in the ministry and as Senior Pastors of New Life Church. Our church is now 18 years old. It started on February 12, 1995. We continue to hold prayer 30 minutes before each service.

CHAPTER 6

Pastoring

We knew the day would come when we would become pastors. The season for our drama team had changed and we found ourselves as youth pastors again to another group of young people. It was 1992 and we began working with young people who God would use in a couple of years to birth Jam Ministries.

I was riding down the road with a friend and my son Carter, who was just a little over a year old. The phone in the vehicle rang.(It was one of the early cell phones that were not portable but mounted in the vehicle.) I answered the phone and it was a Godly woman named Liz Hearn, who had known Bryan and I for years. We had been her children's youth pastors years before. She said "I've been on my face before God and He told me that He is ready for Bryan to be a senior pastor." I said, "Liz we don't see ourselves leaving this area and we don't want to be accused of having an Absalom Spirit and starting a church by stealing the hearts of people away from the church we are attending." She said to me, "Well Rhonda, I have the witness in my spirit that this is His plan for your lives." I thanked her for sharing what she had called to tell me and hung the phone up in the truck. No sooner had I hung up that I heard what seemed to be an audible voice of God. I heard loud and clear,

"To do what I want to do in this city, your husband must become a senior pastor!" I was not familiar with hearing the voice of God in this way. My friend could see from my expression that I had just had a divine encounter. She asked, "Rhonda, what did He say?" Let me teach you from experience; don't be eager to share everything that you hear God speak to your spirit. I did not feel I could say what I had heard to anyone until I told Bryan. He was working the evening shift and it would be hours before he'd be home, so I could tell him what I had heard.

When he got home about 12:30 a.m., I was about to burst to share my first time hearing an audible voice in my spirit. I told him about the phone call from Liz and the voice that followed saying that Bryan would need to become a senior pastor in our city. It's so important to follow the Holy Spirit in your life. As Bryan and I prayed we only felt to share what I'd heard with my mama, and also Linda Dunaway, who had become our spiritual mama. She was the one who had laid hands on us back in 1986 to answer the call on our lives. We also confided in Phillip and Amy who would be getting married the next month in June 1994. These were the only people that we shared with about what the Lord had spoken. We were careful to pray and wait until the Holy Spirit said it was time to share with our pastor what we had heard God say. I had heard God's voice loud and clear on that sunny day in May 1994. We did not feel a release to share it with our pastor until November of that same year. It's so imperative to wait on God's timing in everything we do.

We made an appointment with our Pastor, Cesar Brooks, to share the vision God had given us. When we walked into our meeting,

Pastor Cesar said, "Before you say anything, I need to tell you that I've been on my face before God. He's told me that whatever you are here to meet with me about that I'm to release you and bless you." We shared what we believed the vision that God wanted us to run with was. We told him that we wanted to start a youth church that would meet on Sunday and Wednesday nights only. We had noticed that out of the 100 teens in our youth group about 70 came from non-church families and were in youth group as a result of being invited by a church going friend. We told Pastor Cesar we would continue our attendance on Sunday mornings. We left the meeting with such an excitement, knowing we had waited on God's timing to share the vision we felt He had given us. Bryan said that day as we were riding home that he felt like Abraham, after patiently enduring he obtained the promise (Hebrews 6:13-15 KJV).

We shared with the other four that had been our prayer partners over this new ministry that we now had the GO from our pastor to launch this new youth church. Let me say here, and we were serious about this, Bryan and I know that God is a God that moves in authority and He had made Pastor Cesar our pastor. If our pastor had not blessed this ministry, we would not have launched it, no matter how badly we wanted to. We truly believe that because we did this God's way and had the blessing of our pastor that this has been one reason we have not had church splits and other churches started in rebellion from our ministry. We know that we have not sown rebellion therefore the devil has no place to cause us to reap rebellion.

CHAPTER 7

Our Very First Building

This November night was extremely exciting for our future. Bryan went to work that night at his secular job on the midnight shift. I really wasn't sleepy because I realized that the prophetic word from April 1988 was about to come to pass, well at least the part of the word I have shared thus far. We had made an appointment to look at a building for our future youth church after we had our pastor's blessing to start this ministry. We were told the building would be $4,000 a month to rent. While in prayer the night before going to see this property, I heard very clearly that our first building would be $1200 a month. I shared that with Bryan when he got off work the next morning. He said to me, "Do we need to go and see the building we have an appointment for since its $4,000?" I said, "Yes, I feel that it's part of His plan to go ahead and look." We were uncertain if we needed to tell the real estate agent that we would be starting a youth church. We had told him we were planning a youth center with video games and pool tables. Bryan had shared that part of the vision with the real estate agent. Our son was a little under 2 at the time and was with Bryan, Phillip, and I looking at this property. Carter had walked a little bit away from me and as I was going to get him, I heard the spirit of God say to tell Bryan to share with this agent about the youth church. Thank God my husband trusts that I hear. He said to the agent, "We are actually looking for a property to have a youth church along with the youth center with video games." The agent said to him, "I have a perfect building. It's $1200 and all you have to do is move in and turn the key." No renovations and the exact amount I had heard! This was exciting to know God hears and answers prayer.

We went to see a former fitness center on Lake Olmstead, and it was truly a perfect fit! We began procedures with planning and zoning and in January 1995, we had the go ahead to occupy this property. On the Sunday morning of February 12, 1995, our pastor put us on stage and said, "This is Bryan and Rhonda Matthews and tonight they will be launching a new youth church called JAM Ministries." He blessed us and said, "If you speak against them or the ministry, you will be speaking against God."

Doing things God's way is truly the only way to walk in the favor and blessings that I will share in this book. I want you to know, that none of these promises would have happened had we not taken prayer very serious and prayed in His will for our lives. I had heard Kenneth Hagin quote John Wesley, "It seems God can do nothing in the earth unless someone prays." So many people take the attitude whatever He wants will happen. If that were true there would be no one unsaved because He desires all men to be saved. Prayer for you and I is cooperating with the will of God and helping to facilitate His plans and purposes in the earth.

Back to this youth church, God gave the name JAM Ministries to Bryan. JAM stood for Jesus Always Moving. We were set to start this exciting youth church with a group of young people who loved

God with every part of their being. The only problem was that most of these awesome young people had no jobs or at best part time jobs. They were mostly high school and college students. We had taught them the principle of tithing and they were a group that was passionate about obeying His Word. Bryan continued to work his secular job which was shift work. He made a very good salary. We felt we were to still tithe to our church that launched us and we attended there on Sunday mornings. We heard the Lord speak to us to give offerings personally to JAM and to know that He was our source. We also felt to put in affect as a ministry one of the biggest keys that we credit to the success of our church besides our commitment to always have prayer at every service. This key was to tithe 10% of the money that came into our ministry. We sent that 10% weekly to the church that launched us. Many people would have thought we were a few bricks shy of a load to take 10% from the amount that wasn't even enough to pay our monthly $1200 rent plus utilities. We are firm believers that whatever God orders He pays for. We also wanted to have integrity as a ministry to always pay our monthly bills before their due date. And praise God He was faithful!

CHAPTER 8

Supernatural Multiplication

We thank God that He was faithful to His Word. We had become familiar with this scripture:

> "Now may He who supplies seed to the sower, and bread for food, supply and multiply the seed you have sown and increase the fruits of your righteousness." (2 Corinthians 9:10 NKJV)

Our ushers would count the offerings and write the amount they counted on a paper and place the money in a little black microphone bag. (We were high cotton!) Usually the offerings were between two and three hundred a week, which would just barely cover our monthly rent much less the utilities. We were still faithful to take 10% of each offering and send it to the church that had launched our ministry. We knew if we honored the principles in God's Word that they would not fail us. We always had more than enough to pay every monthly expense and continued to sow as a ministry. I don't recall exactly how or when I started praying for multiplication. I remember Pastor Phillip teaching the young people on tithes and offerings and I'd hear him say, "God is into addition and multiplication; He's not into subtraction and division." I just recall having an unction to tell the ushers to count the money and write the total. Then I would take that little black microphone bag and pray for multiplication. It was supernatural! I would count the money and write the amount I had counted. Then I would compare the amount I got to what the ushers had counted and written as the amount. I was so excited to see God was honoring my faith on multiplication and addition. It became expected for the amount I counted to double from the original count. The ushers said, "You are making it look like we can't count." I said, "No way, we are all seeing God multiply the finances supernaturally!"

It wasn't long until Julie Brown (Arrowood), who had started this ministry with us and who was also a teller at our bank, decided to get in on this multiplication faith for finances. She would tell me to write the amount that I had counted and before opening that little microphone money bag, she would pray and ask God to multiply the finances again when she counted. Was it crazy faith? It was so exciting to see that the money had usually doubled again from the first multiplication! This was God's ministry and He was showing us that He was able to do exceeding, abundantly; above all we could dare ask or think! I truly would not take anything for those days that we learned to whole heartedly trust in the Lord with all our heart and lean not on our own understanding.

As I said earlier in this book, we began JAM Ministries on February 12, 1995. Bryan still worked shift work at his secular job. He did all the preaching unless he was working the evening shift. When Bryan was working, Pastor Phillip preached the Word. I led the music, and that was also an act of faith. I'm not sure how I knew to get musicians together and have a band produce a sound when I could not, and still do not, read any music. Remember the prophecy I shared earlier that I would lead worship in the House of God? I knew that I could carry a tune and I loved His presence, but that was about all that qualified me to lead a worship team. Eighteen years later I'm still in awe that the Lord has allowed me the privilege of leading His people in worship. One of my husband's favorite sayings is: you staff your weaknesses.

God had stirred the heart of a young lady named Amy Sisler (Herrington) to serve me and help with our son when he was a baby. Amy was also majoring in music in college. She was the gift that God brought into my life over twenty years ago. She still serves along side of me to make the music I desire a reality.

I can't thank God enough for giving me a team of psalmists and musicians who know what they are doing! Where there is unity He commands a blessing. That is in His Word. If we do our part in keeping the unity, then the commanded blessing is a given. Bryan and I can honestly say that in all our years of pastoring, we have not had to deal with prideful and arrogant musicians or singers.

We started JAM, Jesus Always Moving, with Bryan and me as senior pastors and Phillip and Amy Maxwell as our associate pastors. Every ministry needs armor bearers like Phillip and Amy Maxwell. They labored in prayer with us to birth this ministry and together the four of us have had the time of our lives stewarding this great ministry God entrusted to us.

CHAPTER 9

Stepping Out in Faith

There are no words to describe how awesome it was to see these young people and young adults so in love with the Lord and so faithful to help us build this wonderful work for the Lord. As I said earlier, we knew the power and importance of prayer and made sure to have prayer 30 minutes before each service. These young people were so excited to be able to pray in His plans and purposes that it wasn't long before two homes were opened every Monday night for prayer. Such hunger was birthed for the things of the Spirit. These young people were growing into power houses for Jesus.

One of our proudest moments as a spiritual dad and mom was during the first year of ministry. In October, we had a Judgment House Drama. The commitment these young people had to make for it was above and beyond. We have always as a ministry impressed upon our partners that He deserves excellence. The world is known for giving their best and we stressed to them that He truly deserves us to give Him our best. This Judgment House required weeks of preparation, and those involved gave 100%.

The week that we would open the Judgment House drama to our community just happened to be the same time that Bryan, Phillip,

Amy and I were at a conference. We flew home from Colorado on October 30th just in time to see one of the local TV stations doing wonderful coverage of our young people in this Judgment House. To say we were proud was an understatement!

After the TV crew had left, I remember wanting to walk through with a group that was waiting to go through the various scenes. I had been through several moving scenes and was standing in front of the drunk driving scene when I heard that same audible voice in my spirit that had spoken to me a year and half earlier. (The voice that said, "To do what I need to do in this city, your husband will become a senior pastor.") This time I don't think I was as prepared as I'd like to have been for what I was hearing. I heard in my spirit, and it was oh so loud and clear, "I've asked Bryan to lay down his secular job. It's his choice, but the grace will not be on him to pastor and work his secular job." I would love to be able to write that this was a beautiful moment, that I had heard His Voice speak personally to me again, and that I was thrilled. I said I'd like to be able to write that. I began to weep. Most of the people in the group thought I was being touched by the scene, which I might say was oh so powerful. However, I was hearing that God had talked to my husband and all I could think was that I had to find Bryan and see if what I'd heard was right.

I rushed out to find him and told him I needed to talk to him. He looked at me and said that we would talk when we got home. You need to understand, I'm not in the habit of telling my husband that I need to talk to him and he was certainly not the type that would say it can wait till we get home. Before I realized it, I blurted out,

"I think God told me that He's asked you to lay down your secular job." Bryan looked at me and said, "He did tell you that!" What? "Bryan, how did you know?" He looked at me and said, "Because He told me earlier this week at the conference that the grace would no longer be on me to pastor and work my secular job." Then Bryan added, "I said, God, then you tell Rhonda!" I should have been thinking wow, what a confirmation! Shouldn't I, who had watched God multiply offerings supernaturally for the last ten months, be thrilled? Yes, I should have been, but I acted quite the opposite. Maybe this happened to me so someone reading can learn from my faith flop. If you know me, you know that I'm an extremely optimistic person, so my behavior was shocking to me!

When we got home that night I asked Bryan if maybe God meant for him to just work days and fewer hours at his secular job or could he maybe go to work with his brother Bob who owned his own business. Bryan said, "You heard what God said." Then he looked at me and said, "Where is my little woman of faith?" I said, "I don't know. She's gone!" The fact that I had heard God speak so clearly just hours earlier was one thing, but 8 years earlier I had heard Him say that one day Bryan would be in full time ministry. I should have been thrilled that I was hearing God speak so accurately about our future! The question came. Did Bryan have a pension plan? I must say this was a moment in my life that I surprised myself and it took me a couple of weeks to get my spirit settled. One thing I thank God for is my amazing rock of a husband. The only choice for him was obedience to what God had spoken to him to do.

Maybe if I tell you where we were living at the time, it would make me seem self-justified. (No, I don't think so but for good measure I'll share it anyway.) We had built a really nice home on a beautiful lake and had not even lived there a year when we felt we should put it on the market. It sold pretty fast. Bryan and I had looked at property to build again but never had the peace about purchasing anything. We figured that we'd continue to look around and find something that would look and feel right for our new home. We had sold our home, got out of debt, and had no idea where we were going to live. Bryan's Mamaw had a home behind his parents that she was no longer staying in. This could work for a short season until we could find the house He had planned for us.

This short season was about to be rewritten. With Bryan not receiving a salary, we were going to have to really live by faith. Imagine that, a faith church with pastors that live by faith! It doesn't take long to go through a savings when you have a wife and son and no weekly check. I could talk to you about faith. The very first Bible verse I taught my son when he was just a little over a year old was "Without faith it's impossible to please Him." (Hebrews 11:6a KJV) Carter would do the little motions and those words that he sang to me resonated in my spirit. I wanted to be able to please God and the language He understands and moves for is faith. I was getting this resolved in my head and began to take baby steps but at least they were steps forward. I have always loved lipstick, I didn't wear the over the top priced kind, but now with no salary I was going to have to really budget. I began to wear Wet and Wild lipstick. I had to use my faith for that $1 tube!

I know you are wondering how long my faith crisis lasted? It was not longer than a couple of weeks. There is a suggestion I have for those who have had their faith tested in any area: stay with what you know. The Word of God is your faith food. I love Jude verse 20, "But you, beloved, building yourself up on your most holy faith, praying in the Holy Spirit." The Apostle Paul wrote, "I thank my God that I speak with tongues more than you all." (I Corinthians 14:18 NKJV) I'm a firm believer in, if you work the Word, the Word will work for you! I began the discipline of praying in the Holy Spirit daily to build my faith up. Faith is like a muscle, you can cause it to grow.

Bryan, as I told you, is an amazing man. He would want you to know that he too has had faith blocks. There would be times when he would go into the sanctuary and could do nothing but cry. He had a wife and a son but no salary. He would wonder, "God, have I totally missed it?"

CHAPTER 10

Finding the Promised Land

Where faith is concerned, you never arrive. You continue to grow your faith. We were renting our building for church on a month to month basis. We knew at any time the building could sell and we would have only one month to be out of the property. Bryan and I were away visiting friends and in my morning prayer time I heard that the building we were having our services in had just sold. I told Bryan what I'd heard and he said, "Ok, that's fine." He began to pray and confess, "We are blessed coming and going." He said that if God could give us this first building, He can lead us to our next property and it will be better!

In a few hours, the real estate agent that we rented our building from called and said, "I have some bad news, the building has sold." Bryan surprised him when he said, "We know, when do we need to be out?" The agent said, "You are not upset?" Bryan told him that God already had told us and that He would be faithful to lead us to our next place. Being married to a man of such peace and confidence has made this adventure of faith so exciting! We've all heard the saying, "God is never early. He's never late." It was looking like He could be late this time! We were to be out of our current building in two weeks and we had no idea where we were going.

What I'm about to tell you still amazes me because of what God chose to do in this season. He gave me a very specific vision of a piece of property. It was an open field with a slight hill and a curve sign across the road from the property. I knew that it was somewhere between I-20 and Columbia Road. I told Bryan what I'd seen and we took a drive down I-20 and got off on Belair Road driving toward Columbia Road. This was years ago and Belair Road was not nearly as built up as it is today, but there was not an open field in sight. Bryan suggested we get back on 1-20 and go to the next exit. We had never been on Exit 190 (Lewiston Road) and it felt like it was in the middle of nowhere! We got off the exit heading toward Columbia Road. About a mile down on the left was the field that I'd seen in a vision and it was for sale! The slight hill was there and the curve sign across the road. God is into details. You may be thinking how is an open field going to work for a church in just two weeks? Let me tell you I've just written that God is into details; well it's the details He thinks you need to get you moving in the right direction. Yes we were going to still need a building but my rock of a husband was living out, "Be anxious for nothing, but in everything by prayer and supplication, with thanksgiving, let your request be made known to God." (Philippians 4:6 NKJV)

When we saw the property, we pulled over in front of it. Bryan got out of the truck and stood at the edge of the property praying. Carter was just about 3, so I sat in the truck with him while his dad stood there praying. After several minutes of sitting there, a policeman came up and said that a neighbor had called him about a suspicious vehicle pulled over in front of this field. Bryan told him that he was a pastor and was just praying about whether to purchase this land. The officer went back to his car with Bryan's driver license to check him out. A few minutes later he returned and said, "Well you are who you said you were." Then the officer said, "I can't say that I've ever been called to someone who was just praying about whether he should buy land or not".

Now remember, in two weeks we would not have a building to meet in. My husband continued his prayer, "we are blessed coming and blessed going," and the Lord did not fail us. Our ministry found a new home on 2805 Wylds Road and it was a bigger building. Our friend Cathie Richards, that was a real estate agent, asked the owners to let us have it for $1,000 a month. My husband's faith and prayer had produced a bigger building, in a better location, for $200 a month less. Our first two buildings for ministry were fitness centers. We were excited that we would be getting people spiritually fit in these former fitness centers.

Now back to the land on Exit 190. After prayer, we felt it was God's will to purchase this property. I heard the Lord say that this piece of property had been dedicated to the Lord and that the owner was a Godly man who always dreamed of building a church on this site. Bryan and I got to know one of the grandsons who at this time was an older gentleman. Mr. Kelly told us that his grandfather had been a Baptist preacher and that as he plowed those fields he would envision a church built there one day.

CHAPTER 11

Sowing and Reaping

"Where God guides, He provides." This was more than just a cute spiritual saying to us. We knew He had led us to that property and now He would show us how to purchase it. My husband believes very strong in seed time and harvest. We were a very young ministry, right at a year old, and still mostly young people. God put in Bryan's heart to sow four seeds of $250 a piece to ministries that were in a building project. We only had $1,000 and that's all God asked for. This was a step of faith and total dependence on Him. Remember Bryan no longer had the security of his secular job to fall back on. The Lord had spoken to him in October of 1995 and by January of 1996 he had walked away from his very secure job. I heard a quote from Rodney Howard Brown that said, "I'd rather be a wet water walker than a dry boat sitter." Out on the water we were walking and trusting God to perform His Word for us.

The land on Lewiston Road could be owner financed. We just needed the $10,000 down payment. Bryan wrote out the checks to those four ministries and in less than a week we had received $13,000 back on our $1,000 seed. The sources God used to bless us had never sown into our ministry before. We were living proof of Luke 6:38 which says, "Give and it shall be given unto you, good measure, pressed down, and shaken together, and running over, shall men give unto your bosom." We had learned by this point that everything starts with a seed. Once we released our seed, He was able to release to us the harvest.

We purchased this land in 1996 and as of this writing February 22, 2013; we have not yet built on this property. Over the years we were able to purchase more adjoining land. Today we have 32 acres of prime real estate on what is now known as "The Gateway" in Columbia County. We had many prophetic words over the years that we couldn't build on the land yet because we would build too small.

About a year into leasing the property on Wylds Road just behind Augusta Mall, we were able to purchase the building. Once it was ours, we began some much needed renovations. We expanded the sanctuary and made room for children's church and nursery. It was now the third year of JAM Ministries and we felt it was time to add a Sunday morning service to our weekly schedule. For the past 3 years, we had Sunday night and Wednesday night services. The only children we had in our ministry were our son Carter, T.J. Kaszas, Lauren and Savannah Brown, and our nephews, Aaron and Austin Matthews.

God had given Bryan the name Jesus Always Moving, JAM as we called it, and now God asked him to change the name. Bryan was given scriptures about, "a new name I will call you." He was reluctant to change the name that we all were very fond of. He did obey and we became New Life Christian Center in 1998. With the name change, families came in which brought in children.

Pastor Amy had never done children's ministry and has often said, "I answered a call I didn't know I had." There is a familiar saying, "God doesn't call the equipped, He equips the called." That was so true for Pastor Amy and so many who would later answer the call and find the equipment or the anointing to do the assignment. We are firm believers in knowing those who labor among you and that the greatest in the kingdom is servant of all. We have had very little internal conflict because we have not placed a novice in a leadership position and we looked for people who followed the example of Jesus, as He was the greatest servant of all.

I did say I'm an eternal optimist but I don't want you to think that the enemy has not whispered things to people to get them out of their place. Because Bryan and I both love people dearly, it hurts our heart when those people are no longer a part of the team. We have said and truly believe this about every church: some people are called to and some are called through. For the most part we've had very little of this type of sifting with leaders because we believe so strongly in an anointed prayer base.

With our new Sunday morning services in full swing we were changing and growing. Our Sunday night services remained the largest attendance for quite some time, but we now had babies and elementary age children. We first added a baby nursery and children's church. In a short time it became necessary to add 3, 4 and 5 year old classes. We were having growing pains but it was so exciting to see new teachers emerge with a passion for children. As we continued on this growth pattern we tore out walls and made room for more nurseries and even youth rooms. The youth church now needed youth pastors. We really were a Family Church.

CHAPTER 12

Tuesday Prayer Pushers

As we grew we began to add additional staff besides Bryan and I and Phillip and Amy. During this time I began to have a desire to add more prayer times than just prayer before our church services. I felt to start a Tuesday prayer time near the lunch hour. My instructions from the Lord were to teach on prayer and then pray. I am a firm believer in the spirit of prayer being caught. Jesus' disciples asked Him to teach them to pray. I had a Godly praying mama and knew many Godly women that could really pray. I gleaned from them and also found myself crying out for Him to teach me to pray.

In James 5:16, the Word says, "The effectual fervent prayer of a righteous man availeth much." As I obeyed His instructions, I would read over and over John 14, 15 and 16. I would read how Jesus said the Holy Spirit would be a teacher and I very innocently took the word to be true. I asked the Holy Spirit to teach me to pray, to be my helper in prayer, my advocate. Whatever the Word said He would be I wanted that in my life.

I had begun to notice different Godly women wearing a Star of David necklace. Although I knew it had something to do with Israel that was about all I knew. I knew our spiritual mama, Linda, loved Israel and had even been there. I still find this to be most interesting of how I began to pray for the Jewish people and Israel.

If we were ever traveling on a night when there might be church, I would look in the phone book and see if there was a church nearby and their service times. We were in Florida, it was a Wednesday, and I wanted to go to church. Pastor Amy, my Mama and Wendy were all with me. We found a church and went in. Instead of a regular service with worship and preaching, they were having a prayer meeting. I guess I must have seen a prayer meeting, but where I grew up in my denominational church, prayer meeting meant regular service. It certainly wasn't what I'd call a prayer meeting. Maybe at the end of the service we heard prayer requests but I don't recall ever praying at a prayer meeting as I was growing up. Go figure! Back to the prayer meeting that we had just walked into at this church in Florida.

We sat down and joined in prayer as others were praying in the Holy Ghost. I noticed that a man walked past us several times as we sat there praying in our Heavenly language. He would walk past us also praying in the spirit. After a while, this man asked the entire group to come up front and pray for specific things they had on a list. All four of us joined in the circle and this man, who I later found out, was one of the pastors assigned people things to pray for. I found it so surprising that he asked my mom to pray for one of the things on the list and then I really couldn't believe that he asked me to pray for Israel. Me, pray for Israel? Yes, it was all part of His plan somehow. I experienced the Holy Spirit as my teacher. I found myself praying things about the peace of Jerusalem and Israel being the apple of His eye, what I heard coming from my mouth, rather my heart surprised me! The pastor said, "This girl has a heartbeat for Israel." I truly believe he spoke over me a word that gave me a passion to pray for Israel.

As I already said, Pastor Amy was with me on this night along with Mama and Wendy. When we got into the car to go home Amy said, "How did you know what to pray for Israel? If they had called on me I might have said 'thank you Lord for the nation of Jerusalem and the city of Israel.'" That may sound humorous, but we were just being taught by Him to pray for Israel. I told them all that I don't know how I knew what to pray. He gave me the words and from that night until now I can say I have a heartbeat for Israel. I made a promise to God that every Tuesday in corporate prayer we would pray for the Prime Minister of Israel and the peace of Jerusalem. There is no greater joy than to be a watchman on the wall.

One Tuesday in prayer many years ago, we began to pray about a missile not hitting an Israeli aircraft. We prayed until we felt a release. Imagine how excited we were to hear on Thanksgiving Day just two days later that a missile had been fired and a passenger on an Israeli airline saw it go right past his window. Prayer is truly a Holy Occupation! The Creator of the Universe needs you and I to take the prayer assignments He gives us very serious. Someone's life depends on our obedience in prayer. Let me tell you prayer is not some somber woe is me time. It is fun, adventurous, and most fulfilling. If there is an emergency that He moves on you to pray about, that too is fulfilling because it shows He trust you to pray the person or situation through. What an awesome privilege.

One of the greatest prayer habits I ever put into practice was taking a journal into our corporate prayer times and having someone write down and date what we were praying about. This takes a special anointing on someone and I prefer that person to have legible penmanship. A seasoned journalist develops a pattern to write in a way that makes future references in the journal easy to read. I thank God for this gifted person! I have so many journals today and I know they represent years of heartfelt prayers.

CHAPTER 13
Finding Sugar Creek

Over the years, Bryan and I have received many prophetic words. The apostle Paul told his spiritual son Timothy to "wage a good warfare with the prophecies concerning him." (I Timothy 1:18) Bryan and I are firm believers that God will speak to us through His Word and His Spirit most often. Jesus said that His sheep would know and recognize His voice. We do know that He gave the 5-fold ministry for the equipping of the saints. One of those gifts is the office of the Prophet.

When Bryan obeyed the Lord and left his secular job, we were living in his mamaw's place. We thought we had moved in just for a few months until we could find the next place we wanted to buy or build. We certainly did not realize at the time that He was getting us in a place that we could more easily obey Bryan stepping away from his secure job and pastoring full time. After a few years of not having our own home, I was getting stir crazy and ready to nest. It was 1999 and I had heard a teaching from Jerry Savelle called, What would make 99 Divine? I thought my own home would be great! Jerry encouraged those listening to the message to make a list. It was not a name it, claim it message. This message was full of faith. The reason he encouraged you to make a list is so you would know when you found your promise. I prayed and made my list. In the natural it was not possible for us to afford what I had put on my list. I'm going to include my list here because I feel like someone reading needs this faith booster. The home we had sold a few years earlier was 2300 square feet and on a lake and we had a pool. I began my list with...

1) A home a little bigger than 2300 square feet, because God you promote and I want it a little bigger!

2) I want it to be on the water again

3) I'd like a pool again, but I'd like a little shape to this pool

4) A big master bedroom and closet

5) A pull down ironing board

6) I'd like drawers in some of the kitchen cabinets

Maybe you are thinking that's a bit materialistic, but it was what was in my heart and what I felt my faith had developed to believe for. God's Word says, "If you being evil know how to give good gifts to your children, how much more will your Heavenly Father give the Holy Spirit to those who ask Him." (Luke 11:13 NKJV) Our son Carter knew his earthly parents loved giving him good gifts and in comparison to God, we were evil? So of course we knew our Heavenly Father was ready to give us our heart's desire for a specific home.

A very close prophetic friend, Ed Traut, was having lunch with us and looked at me and said "Rhonda, the Lord has a house for you, it's wooden and has a big porch, there are lots of trees and it backs up to the water." Then he said, "It's on a frontage road that used to be dirt and was recently paved, but you will not hear the noise of the interstate." All I could picture in my mind was a country house with a wraparound porch. Had I waited this many years for a country farm house? My mom would love that but I wanted something more contemporary.

A few weeks went by and I began to try and figure out how I could get me a house. Couldn't we just build somewhere on the church property on Lewiston Road? Maybe I didn't need the house to be as big. There were some trees on the church land and the property next to ours had a pond. We could build near the trees and maybe we could see the pond on the land near us. And about the frontage road that he prophesied, maybe because Ed was from South Africa it was a language barrier. Maybe Lewiston Road would be what he called a frontage road and of course it used to be dirt! Now, I just had to sell Bryan on my plan to build our home on church land. I mean, we were pastors and it could be our parsonage like you see many churches have.

You may be thinking, what about your list for what would make 99 divine? Why was I so willing to cast away my confidence about my home? Thank God for children. The Bible says a little child will lead them. One day, we had a family day and Easter Egg Hunt at our Lewiston Road property. After the activities, I left with Carter, who was 6, and Savannah Brown, who was 8. We lived in Hephzibah at this time and it was not anywhere near this area. I remember as we were driving down Lewiston Road, heading toward I-20, that I noticed a for sale by owner sign at Sugarcreek neighborhood. I turned in that street and Carter looked up and saw a real estate sign with the agent's last name Carter. He said, "Mom, stop! That's our house. It has my name on it!" Of course I stopped. Childlike faith is contagious! There was an information sheet with details about the home. Carter jumped out and got one and I could not believe what I was reading. Everything on my home list was there! Even a lazy "L" shaped pool. The only obstacle I could see was the price. I remember driving away thinking, could this really be our home? I never did find the for sale by owner house that I had originally turned in to see.

When Bryan got home that evening after doing major renovations in our church on Wylds Road, (we had just purchased this property and we were firm believers that if we take care of God's House, then He'd take care of our house), I showed Bryan the information sheet on the home. Carter was fully persuaded it was already ours. We had a real estate friend that could hook up with our faith, Cathie. She made us an appointment to see the home. After going in, we found everything on my list in this house. This felt so right, but how God, I wondered. Bryan had begun to make a small salary by this time, but there was no way we could in the natural afford this home.

Ed Traut was back in town visiting us even though he had been with us just a month before. I was eager to show Ed the house that fit my list and see if God showed him anything for us. As we were driving down I-20, Ed looked over at a frontage road and said,

"Rhonda, the Lord shows me your home is on that road, "Whoa!!!"
I said "Ed, the house we are going to show you, is on that road".
He said, "Is it wooden?" I said, "Yes". He said, "Does it have a big
porch?" I said, "Yes but it's on the back of the house not on the
front." He said, "Did the Lord say it has a big front porch?" I said,
"No, I just assumed it was a wraparound country porch." Then Ed
asked me, "Are there lots of trees?" Again my answer was, "Yes." His
last question was, "Does the house back up to water?" "Yes!" Ed
said, "It's your home, pursue it!" At this point it would it be a lack
of faith if I asked how. After this powerful, specific prophecy, we
were fully persuaded with Carter that this was indeed our home.

There was one slight obstacle. The house was under contract. We
were not the ones who had put this contract on it. How could this
be? I had my list and a prophecy about this house. Now what?

Several weeks went by and as far as we knew, our house was sold
to someone else. One Sunday afternoon, after a nap, I awoke with
a tune and words, "All things work together for good to those
who love the Lord and who are called according to His purpose.
Although I'm able to see, sometimes it's not very clear, I must never
allow my heart to be in fear. There'll be things I don't understand
but when I trust you Lord and hold to your plan I know that all
things work together....." I told Bryan, "The house is ours, I just
know it." Then I shared with him the song God had given me. I
heard a word of knowledge that the people who had the contract
on the house would back out of it and that I would hear these
words, "The strangest thing happened." I told Bryan this too. He
said, "Well, we are going to offer them a lot less money for them

making us wait so long." What confidence my husband had in me that I'd heard from God about the house.

I was so full of expectation that we would receive word about the house that night that I gave my pager to Pastor Amy in case Cathie paged to tell me the good news. When I was done leading praise and worship, Pastor Amy said, "Cathie paged you and I called her back. She said the other people had backed out of the contract on the house and the strangest thing happened." They were told by their insurance agent that they would have to put a fence around the pool, so they decided to back out of the contract. God caused all things to work together for good. Due to some hail damage on the roof we were able to get the house for $40,000 less than our original offer a month earlier.

Another house came on the market during the time we had to wait for this promise house. It was on the same street and was also on the water. Cathie took us to see it. It was a lovely home, but it didn't have all the things on my list. I prayed that God would let the people who had put the contract on the house I felt was ours see this house and fall in love with this lovely home. It would be several years before I had a confirmation that they had indeed purchased that very house. A real estate agent said to me, "I had a pretty firm contract on that house." I said to this agent, "Did they buy the house down the street that came on the market after they had the contract on my house?" She said, "Yes they did. How did you know?" I said, "Because I prayed for God to let them see that house since I knew the other one was ours." She was truly amazed that I believed God could do anything! Then she said, "And He did!"

CHAPTER 14

Growing Pains

New Life Christian Center was growing and we were running out of space. These were good growing pains. We had our property on Lewiston Road but still did not feel the release to build there yet. We had purchased additional property that we could expand on at our current location. We were not sure if we would need to use that space for parking soon. There was a business that had a huge parking area near our church that was not opened on Sundays. A good bit of our church parked there. The business sold and Bryan had concerns if the new business going in would be open on Sundays and we would no longer be able to use those parking places. He called the real estate agent, Ann Davis, which had sold to the new business.

He asked Ann if we could maybe lease some of the parking from the new owners. She told him that it would not be a problem for our church to continue to park there. That was great news. Now we could expand our church on the little piece of property behind our building. Ann asked Bryan if he had ever considered the former Circuit City property. Bryan told her they were asking 2 million dollars and that it would cost at least 2 million for renovations. If we were going to be spending that kind of money, then we would probably be using it toward developing our property on Lewiston Road. Bryan made this phone call on the Wednesday before Thanksgiving in 2003. Ann told him that she had been contacted by a company on Monday that wanted her to help them find a church to put in that property. They would buy the property and donate it to the church they chose. She told Bryan to come to her office on the Monday after Thanksgiving for a phone interview with the company executives.

I remember right where I was when I got the phone call from Bryan about this potential miracle. He was so excited and our faith was so stirred because as I've said many times already in this book, we were waging warfare with a specific part of that first prophecy from April 18, 1988. There was a word to us that land and property would be granted and given over to us in the years to come for our ministry. This same prophetic word had that I would lead worship in the House of God and that Bryan would be made a pastor. Those parts of the word had come to pass in 1995 and Bryan and I had gotten really serious about waging warfare over property being granted or given to our ministry. Now he was being asked to come for a phone interview. Monday could not get here soon enough!

Bryan went to Ann's office for the phone interview and he felt it went good. Ann called later that day and said the company executives from Hobby Lobby told her to not look any further. They loved Bryan and wanted to purchase this property for our church!

We thank God for principles that were instilled in us to pay our bills on time and keep our word. We had started a place called The Rock for young people. It was a very expensive lease and only being opened on Friday and Saturday nights did not cover all the expenses. We honored our lease even though we closed The Rock a few months before our lease was up. Imagine how this day of our miracle property could have been different if we had not been Christians with integrity? Was it a test of our character? I think so. Praise God that Ann Davis could recommend my husband and New Life for this Circuit City Property.

Now comes the question I bet everyone is thinking, "Is this too good to be true?" Bryan asked the Green Family, "I don't mean to sound ungrateful, but this seems almost too good to be true. Can you give me a name of someone else that you've done this for?" They were most gracious and gave us several names of churches and organizations. One just happened to be a church in Myrtle Beach, South Carolina and we just happened to be going there in January to pray with some of our pastors. They were most gracious people and totally understood our inquiry. We went to meet the pastors of this blessed church who had just received a piece of amazing property from Hobby Lobby. They said they too had been skeptical if this was for real. Yes, it was for real. Hobby Lobby is a benevolent business who has held to a high Godly standard in business and they buy property all over for ministries and hospitals. Their story is amazing and I urge you to support their business. At the time they purchased the former Circuit City property for us, they did not even have a business in the Augusta area.

As I write this, I'm still amazed that God moved on their hearts to give property to us. They still, as of this writing, have never met us and it's been ten years. What a Godly family and company! As I am writing this book in February 2013, please pray for this company as they have made a stand morally to not be pushed into providing certain health care coverage that goes against their core beliefs. What made our country great are God fearing citizens. What will get our country back on track is God! We need God fearing praying people "who are not ashamed of the Gospel (the good news) for it is the power of God unto salvation," (Romans 1:6 KJV).

Because of the battle that Hobby Lobby has had with our government, maybe I'm on a soap box, but this is a book He asked me to write. I can't help but think of the scripture in Matthew 5:13 (NKJV) that says, "If salt has lost its flavor what's its use?" Salt is a preservative. Thank you, Hobby Lobby family, for being that preservative. May men and women rise up and follow this company's Godly example and take a stand for righteousness and holiness. Hobby Lobby is a company that has taken their blessings and provision and invested it all over the world. We are just one of the many ministries they have blessed. Can you imagine the eternal fruit they have produced?

CHAPTER 15

Our Miracle Building

It would take a lot of hard work from our partners to take this former Circuit City property and make it into a beautiful church for His glory. I am married to my favorite preacher, but found out that this amazing man had another gift. Yes, pastors need to be visionaries for their churches, but my husband could look at a building that looked nothing like a church and use every bit of space to create a state of the art ministry for children, youth, and adults. This property was 15 acres and over 100,000 square feet. A big portion of that square footage had not been used in years except by the pigeons! When I say my husband is a visionary, I mean he's a visionary.

We have always believed in wise stewardship and Bryan has received numerous prophecies that he would have a hammer and nail in his hand. (Is there something in every man that just enjoys knocking things down?) Demolition was quite the process in this huge property we were blessed with. This was not a project that women or children were excluded from. If you had a heart and mind to work, then you were welcome to come and build Gods house.

As I'm writing, I'm reminded of two prophetic voices that have spoken in our lives over the years. One is Jan Painter. She was the first that spoke over us that we could not yet build on our Lewiston Road property because we would build too small. God knew this Circuit City property would be in our future through the miraculous circumstances I've described earlier. She also prophesied that every time we increased in natural land we would increase in spiritual territory. Ed Traut, who I have referred to already, said over us that we would never, not be building something for Him. He said as Bryan builds in the natural, he is also building in the spirit. Another prophecy said, "The work will only escalate."

My husband does love to be a part of demolition and construction, but I can honestly say that he's not so busy building God's work without making sure that he is not vulnerable for burnout. Many years ago he said God told him, "Don't build something that is bigger than you are." From that day forward, Bryan has been careful to make sure his daily word and prayer time are top priority.

Maybe you are thinking that this girl's husband must be a super saint? Well, I think so! He is such an unassuming leader that has the heart of a shepherd and would willingly lay down his life for those God has entrusted him with. As of this writing, you can find my husband once again with a hammer and nail in his hand as we are getting ready to occupy yet another property on our journey to get to our Promise Land on Lewiston Road.

The construction on the Circuit City property took more than a year. In June of 2005, we moved our wonderful church family into its new home at 3336 Wrightsboro Road, prime real estate just a mile from our local mall.

We were eager to get into this new building. On Friday before our first Sunday service in June, we were granted from the county the paper we needed to move into our beautiful new church. How were we going to let our people know? Should we still have another service at our Wylds Road location and let everyone know that way? We made the decision to go ahead and meet in our beautiful new facility without any sign out front or real way of letting everyone know we were there. We placed a sign on the door to our former church letting people know where to find us that exciting Sunday morning. This day exceeded our expectations. We were packed and had no idea how the new people found us. This new church would seat many more people and yet it was almost full. Bryan said it was like the movie Field of Dreams…, "if you build it, they will come."

It wasn't long before we were in double services in our much larger sanctuary. Bryan was about to get another hammer and nail in his hand, but first his master mind architectural self would have to draw out what he was seeing for this former pigeon coop portion of the building. By May of 2008, this desolated part of the property was now transformed into the most beautiful sanctuary I had ever seen. Many people have asked us who our interior designers were. We would tell them that it was Bryan, Pastor Amy, and I. I had majored in Fashion Merchandising and had several opportunities by now to pick carpet, chairs, and wall color with two of my favorite people in the world, my husband and Pastor Amy. If Bryan needed a building project fix then I guess I could say this was my fix to be able to use my love for decor and color. It bears repeating again, "Where there is unity, God commands a blessing." We had unity with our Elders and Board. They were so supportive of the vision

God had given our pastor. What a joy to be part of a strife free team!

CHAPTER 16
40 Day Fast

Just as we were preparing to move into our newest sanctuary, I felt that I was to go on my first 40 day fast. I am an extremely graced faster. My husband says when God speaks to him to prepare for a fast, he starts to really get hungry. I realize it is not the norm, but I look so forward to when He speaks to me to fast. It is times of sweet fellowship for me with the Lord. For some reason during a fast, I have the ability to say no to all the demands and activities that can pull a pastor's wife in so many directions. I genuinely love people and want them to feel they are important to me.

While fasting, I have my Bible and journal with me at all times with such anticipation that He will speak to me. One of the things I heard Him speak to me was that Bryan and I needed to go to Israel. A pastor's wife invited me to a special minister's meeting. Pastor Amy and I went to this meeting and of course I was thrilled to hear the preacher speak on prayer. He was from another country and had seen firsthand the power of prayer in his third world country. What he spoke and his humility of heart gave me the desire to go again the next day to the service.

This time my mom and spiritual mom went with me. I have had many prophetic words in my life, but never have I had anyone call my name out. Right in the middle of his message, he stopped and said, "Where is Rhonda?" I'm sitting there thinking, "Did he just call my name?" Yes he had! I went to the front and he said, "What you are doing has God's attention and He is pleased with your sacrifice." He then went on to say things about my love for prayer and the favor of God over our ministry. How thrilling to have the Holy Spirit tell me by name that He appreciates my sacrifice. I love to fast!

During this entire fast everywhere I would turn I would get scriptures about Israel and Zion. Finally, Bryan and I decided it was time for us to visit The Holy Land. We purchased our tickets and immediately had confirmation that this was indeed His timing to go. A Godly pray-er, Maria, who had been in our church from the beginning, told me she had a vision of Bryan and me in Israel two years earlier but felt she needed to share it with me that day. Wow! Talk about confirmation.

The next supernatural sign happened in the prayer room on Sunday morning before our service. My husband is a pastor who believes in prayer and he leads intercessory prayer 30 minutes before the morning service. This particular Sunday, he had prayed in English and was praying in other tongues. After prayer was over, a wonderful couple, Ron and Sandra Jenke, came up to me and told me that Pastor Bryan was speaking in Hebrew as he was speaking in tongues. How exciting! I asked, "What did he say?" Sandra, who is a Messianic Jew, said he was praying for salvation to come to His chosen people, the Jews. I was thrilled to tell her and Ron that we had just purchased our tickets to go to Israel and would be leaving in a couple of weeks. To walk where Jesus walked is the most amazing thing. Truly the Word comes alive as you walk in the land where our Bible was written.

CHAPTER 17

An Invitation to Kenya

As I said in the previous chapter, I'm an unusually graced faster. In January 2010, while on a 3 day fast, Bryan and I received an email inviting us to come to Kenya. It was a really heartfelt request coming from a pastor from Lucky Summer, a slum area right outside of Nairobi. When this email request came, I read it and prayed for this pastor and had no natural desire to go to Kenya. We receive invitations to go to many third world countries. I did not know this was going to be an invitation that we would accept.

About a week had passed since reading the email to come to Kenya. I was away praying while on this fast. There is such truth to what Jesus said about prayer and fasting. I like the fact that Jesus expected His followers to develop these healthy habits. He said "When you pray, when you fast." So as I'm praying about different things this January afternoon, I hear very clear in my spirit, "Rhonda, that invitation to Kenya was from Me. I need you to answer this pastor." My thoughts were, can we just send him support Lord? When I returned home, I looked up this pastor's email to us. The first thing I noticed was that it was dated January 21st. Why had I not noticed that day before? It's my husband's birthday.

I re-read the email and was particularly moved by the fact that this pastor said, "We are like the Macedonians asking you to come over and help us." Obedience is a key to breakthrough and blessing. I responded to his email. My question was how did you happen to find our church? He told me that he had an all night prayer meeting when God spoke to him, "New Life." I was so excited! This could be a pastor after our own heart. He was having a prayer meeting. No wonder this invitation was so important to the Lord! We spent the next few months communicating by email.

There were some young people who had heard about our invite to Kenya. With our love for teens, we talked about taking a trip as soon as school was out for summer. Bryan felt that wisdom would be to first send spies into the land. Pastor Phillip has always been more than willing to travel to uncharted territory. He loves to go to the nations.

Pastor Phillip and Todd Wilson left for this unknown adventure in May. They were gone for days and neither of their wives had heard from them. What was most unusual was I had not received any emails or phone calls from my new pastor friend in Kenya. These guys are our traveling spies and we aren't getting in reports from the land. Fearful thoughts tried to knock on my door. Had I missed it? I had felt in my spirit that this was a God invitation. Why had we not heard from them? The pastor from Kenya had been in touch with us every few days prior to the guys going to Kenya. The Word says to take every thought captive, I really had to do that.

Finally, days into their trip, Pastor Peter called. I was beyond excited to see those long set of numbers come up on my phone. I answered and said, "Where is Pastor Phillip, can I speak to him?" Pastor Peter answered, "He is very tired and resting." Can you imagine the thoughts running through my head? Have we sent them to some place with voodoo and they've done something to them? Crazy how the devil can plant thoughts that produce fear. Pastor Peter reassured me that the guys had been really busy with the long days of travel to villages.

Not only had our fellows not been in touch with any of us, but Kim Meyer had not been in touch with her husband either. Kim was a lady from the USA that had met up with Pastor Phillip and Todd to go on this trip. She and her friend had traveled to Kenya a couple of times before. Pastor Peter had given us her name to talk to her about Kenya. Kim and her friend had helped to raise funds to drill a bore hole and bring water to the village Pastor Peter had grown up in. We were thrilled when Kim said she would be glad to go and introduce our guys to Pastor Peter. As the days passed and no word from Pastor Phillip or Todd, we decided we should call Kim's husband, Jim. He had not heard from Kim either! I asked him, "Was this normal?" He said, "No, she has always contacted me when she arrives in Kenya." Praise God the guys finally called home! It was the end of their trip when we heard from them. They were in love with the Kenyans! We are still not sure why they didn't use Pastor Peter's phone to call home. (I've included the above story so that you can know how Kenya became such a big part of our heart.)

CHAPTER 18

Water for Kenya

The word of God tells us to ask for the nations as our inheritance. Prior to his first trip to Kenya, Pastor Phillip would tell you that he'd ask for Europe. He felt graced for many nations but had not had the pull toward Africa. The pull came and he has fallen in love with the people from Kenya. Praise God I had heard correctly that this was God's invitation back in January on the fast! Pastor Peter, from Kenya, continued to talk to us via email and was anticipating the day he would meet Bryan and I. He felt the Lord had shown him that we would become his spiritual parents. We began to pray about the timing for us to go to Kenya ourselves.

In August of that same year, eight of us went to Kenya. The people and the land were just as our "original spies" had told us. They were some of the sweetest people we had ever met. On a Sunday morning, while traveling to Pastor Peter's church for service, the presence of God came so strong in the vehicle. It was our habit to spend time singing and praying along these Kenyan roads. You could find yourself in a vehicle for many, many hours.

Prophetic words have no expiration date. I've already shared that Bryan and I received our very first prophecy on April 18, 1988. We had seen a big part of that word come to pass. I was leading worship as prophesied and Bryan was pastoring. We had also been given the 100,000 square foot property. Suddenly, I realized Kenya had been part of God's plan for our lives for years. A part of the prophetic word was, "I'm going to send the two of you into a place of service that will shock you! I want to say place and leave it at that, but the Lord said it is a nation that needs you." This was one of those oh my moments! What had just seemed to be an invite to another country, via the email, was a prophetic word about to be fulfilled in our lives. The prophecy went on to say "I'll make you to bring water, not one that cuts water on and off, but water that will run continuously."

As of this writing, we have been in and out of Kenya many times. Our partners have such a passion for Kenya. We have purchased land to build a church in the Lucky Summer Slum area. You would think for the price we had to pay for this land. It was prime real estate in a fancy neighborhood. Our vision is to build a beautiful church, with youth and children facilities. We believe God wants to change the slums for His Glory. This property sets on a hill. My husband prays often, "A city that is set on hill that cannot be hidden." (Matthew 5:14b NKJV)

Our partners also got behind the vision we had to purchase a truck that would drill many wells. This would fulfill the prophetic word that water would run continuously. If you've ever been to any country and see children without water, it breaks your heart. As Christians we aren't called to do everything, but we are called to do something. Bryan has the heart of a true shepherd. His heart's desire is to plant a church in every place we drill a well. Imagine, their deepest need is water. They come to get natural water and have the opportunity to get the Living Water and never thirst again!

At this writing we have nineteen churches in Kenya villages all under Pastor Peter and New Life Church in Kenya. The very first need we saw was the need for a vehicle for Pastor Peter. He had holes in his shoe soles from walking to share the good news. He would have to hire drivers to take him to the villages to check on the pastors and the churches. The level of commitment we've seen in all these pastors has taken a "living sacrifice" to a new level for us.

One village pastor walked 50 miles, one way, to let a fellow pastor know we had purchased bus tickets for all these pastors. We were to be holding a pastor's conference in Nairobi and Pastor John wanted to make sure this village pastor knew that his bus fare was paid. Most of these people have a cell phone, which is how they communicate from one place to another. You can be in a very remote place and yet have a cell phone. This one pastor did not have a phone. Thank the Lord, a fellow pastor was his brother's keeper.

Pastor John is a pastor in a village called Katse. We are so fond of this village and they have an amazing church! Our middle school department raised money to purchase Pastor John a motorcycle. Prior to his blessing, Pastor John, his wife and three boys walked one hour, one way to church.

My prayer is, "God stir me to this level of passion for you!" God continues to confirm our assignment to Kenya. We were donated land near one of the villages to build an orphanage. The privilege to help feed and clothe them has been awesome. Now, we need to take this love to a new level by building them a home with running water and electricity. These precious children have captivated our hearts.

I could write so much more about the work in Kenya. This is a book about prayer, and I have many journals of our prayer times. After having made two trips to Kenya, I found that we had prayed "Kenya" by the spirit in other tongues back in 1998. I'm a firm believer that you can't work in a place unless prayer has gone before you.

CHAPTER 19

Praying Mysteries

My prayer journals represent time invested in following the Holy Spirit and His desires. I've often said the Spirit of Prayer is not taught as much as it is caught. It's a well-known fact you become like who you hang out with. There is nothing I love more than to find people who have a passion to facilitate His purposes on the earth through prayer. I have found that He will raise up companies of pray-ers who have similar prayer assignments.

I know you've heard me say in this book that my mama is my biggest fan. She's been a huge part of my prayer company for years. I remember back in the late 90's she, Pastor Amy, and I would pray together. We would be praying in other tongues and hear English words come out as we were praying. None of us were familiar with this type of praying, however, we all three were following the Holy Spirit in these places. As we noticed these English words being prayed out, we decided that we should write them down. This is where we began to start keeping prayer journals. I cannot recommend this enough. We are still amazed when we look in journals from the same seasons but different years and see that the Holy Spirit has had us pray out many times the exact same spirit led words. Wow! He never ceases to amaze me.

Because Mama, Pastor Amy, and I were not flaky Christians, we trusted He was leading us to pray this way. Even though we had not yet heard anyone else pray English words when praying in other tongues, we felt in our spirit this was right. I have constantly believed in Romans 8:14 (NKJV), "For as many as led by the Spirit of God, they are the sons of God." It wouldn't be long until we were introduced to the ministry of Lynne Hammond and would go to prayer conferences to see men and women praying this same way.

One of my favorite chapters in the Word is 1 Corinthians 2. In this chapter are many verses that bore witness in my spirit:

> "9 But as it is written: Eye has not seen, nor ear heard, nor have entered into the heart of man the things which God has prepared for those who love Him.10 But God has revealed them to us through His Spirit. For the Spirit searches all things, yes, and the deep things of God. 11 For what man knows the things of a man except the spirit of the man which is in him? Even so no one knows the things of God except the Spirit of God. 12 Now we have received, not the spirit of the world, but the Spirit who is from God that we might know the things that have been freely given to us by God. 13 These things we also speak, not in words which man's wisdom teaches but which the Holy Spirit teaches, comparing spiritual things with spiritual. 14 But the natural man does not receive the things of the Spirit of God, for they are foolishness to him; nor can he

know them, because they are spiritually discerned."
(1 Corinthians 2:9-14 NKJV)

In the early days of praying this way, we would write in our journals and say we were praying the mysteries of God. Some of the things we have prayed about for years are still a mystery to us! We just continue to lift those things, whether they are people or places, back to the Lord in prayer.

One such place was Aruba. In August of 2004, we began to notice that we were often praying out the word Aruba. We began to seek the Lord about this. The direction we were getting is that one day we would plant a work there. You can call us innocent or ignorant, but we didn't know at the time where Aruba was at! As I have referred to in this book already when the Holy Spirit wants my attention about something He will cause me to see or hear that thing many times. I'm not famous for human reasoning. If I feel He speaks something to me, I will just trust Him before my brain catches up. Then He is able to use me.

As I said, we were noticing Aruba a lot in the prayer journal. (I've looked up the location by this point.) It is November 2004 and Pastor Amy said, "I feel you and Pastor Bryan will go to Aruba before the year is up." Hmm? That gave us one month. I was leading worship on this November Sunday night and I called on one of our singers, John Fobish, to just lead us in whatever the Spirit was leading. Brother John began to sing in a very island sound. I shocked myself when I said from the stage, "Bryan and I are going to Aruba before the year is over!" Did I really just say that? I hadn't even had the opportunity to filter this through Bryan yet. It's one of those moments that you hear what you are saying and think, can I pick those words back up and put them in my mouth? Well it was out there now and I'm thankful my husband knows I don't just flippantly say things. We got home from church and had on the last 15 minutes of a movie. The flight attendant comes up to a man and says "Your next assignment: the Caribbean, ARUBA." Ok God, we get it, we will go! And go we did in December 2004.

I don't know about you, but when I'm on uncharted paths and they don't look like I had planned, I sometimes think maybe I didn't hear right. That was the case with Aruba. While on the trip, I enjoyed myself but thought, ok I obeyed and that's all He needs me to do here. The final night, He gave me a dream and I knew Aruba would forever be a work that He wanted us to do. In 2005, national attention was on Aruba with the disappearance of Natalie Holloway. Our media encouraged tourist to stay away. We did that for a season, but the stirring for Aruba wouldn't leave. Everywhere I would turn, God would give me a sign that this was His assignment for us.

I was at a ladies conference in Tennessee just after Hurricane Katrina. The speaker got up and said "I had a good word to speak, but God needs somebody to just obey Him and say yes!" She closed her Bible and said, "Now do business with Him." Right there in that church under my breath I said, "Ok Lord, I will go to Aruba!" I'm not expecting Him to share with anyone my YES yet. As we are walking back to our vehicle, my friend, Sarah Kaszas looks at me and says, "Did God make you say YES to Aruba again?" I said, "YES, but shut up!" I don't talk that way. I was maybe trying to make light of this very serious YES! I picked up my cell phone to check voice mails and couldn't believe my ears. Someone had called our church and wanted to talk to me about Aruba. But God, I just told you YES less than ten minutes ago, aren't we moving a bit quick here? I returned the phone call and yes, I had heard right!

One of our partners had an aunt that lived in Mississippi. She had called her niece that morning to tell her that the Lord had woke her up early to pray for her pastor's wife. She said, "The Holy Spirit said that your pastor's wife has an assignment in Aruba." Talk about another quick confirmation! God had moved on a lady that I had never met to pray for me about Aruba. He had a preacher at a conference forego her message to ask people to obey what He's asking. So with a resolve that Aruba was His plan, now what? At this writing we have gone there many times to pray.

In May 2010, we asked our prophetic friend Ed and his wife Louisa to join us in Aruba. Ed travels all over the world and he knew that we prayed for Aruba. However, we had never told him that we had felt we would plant a work there. While talking with him one night at dinner, he said to Bryan and I that he felt we were to start a church there and that we would send a couple from our church to pastor. This is the part that excited us: he said, "This will be the easiest place you've ever won souls." Isn't that our entire purpose for existing, to bring people to God?

It will take a good bit of leg work and prayer to get the ball rolling. At this writing we have been granted the foundation papers which are necessary to have any nonprofit business there. Also, you have to have a local Aruban citizen to be on your board. God has blessed us with a Godly man who is a native Aruban. So now what about the couple that we will send from our church? My husband heard the names, but they weren't married. They weren't even dating yet! Talk about faith. This is why prayer is so important. We did not manipulate this couple. We prayed, "God if this is of you, bring them together." I am happy to write they will be married on April 27, 2013 and will spend their honeymoon in Aruba. They know by the spirit that pastoring in this place is His plan.

CHAPTER 20

No Child Left Behind

The next few years proved to be years where many answered prayers happened. Because we started our church with young people, Bryan and I have always enjoyed getting to spend time with them at youth camp. It was July 2011 and as Bryan and I were driving to camp, I shared with him a scripture that was in my spirit. (Zechariah 6:15 NKJV) The latter part really stood out to me. "And your part in this shall come to pass if you will diligently obey the voice of your God." I was sharing with Bryan that obedience was very important to me and key to receiving the plans from the Holy Spirit.

Camp was called Resonate and the young people were so hungry and really worshipping the Lord. Pastor Eli was laying hands on young people that had come from broken homes. I heard the Holy Spirit speak to me that He was going to hold me accountable if I didn't use my faith for camp land to be released. My husband, as I've already told you, has such a heart of a shepherd. We had been raising money for the land and drilling truck for Kenya. We also had children and youth that wanted to go to camp. If you have rented a camp before, you know they usually charge you a per person rate. We had many partners help these kids and young people raise their money, but what about those that were too shy to ask for donations? One Sunday morning, my husband began to weep as he shared his heart to have our own camp. He said no child would ever be turned away. While he was speaking the Holy Spirit said, "Bryan I am able to do both. You can believe me for money for Kenya projects and camp property." It was settled in his spirit, God was able.

Here I was standing at this youth camp hearing, "Rhonda I'm going to hold you accountable if you don't use your faith for camp land." As soon as the service was over, I found Bryan and told him what I had just heard. He said, "Then get to using it girl!" If you are not fully persuaded that God has exciting adventures awaiting you, I pray you get stirred up with these stories.

About 15 minutes after I had told Bryan what the Lord had said to me, I received a text. Now there is nothing unusual about me getting a text. (I wonder how I communicated before texting!) This text said, "Hey Pastor Rhonda, this is Mellony that you met in Vegas! The Lord says that you and your husband are in a window of opportunity and there are some things that you are to move on now. He's with you! Trust Him to do the impossible! I also see streams of income opening up for both you personally and the ministry! I'm so excited to hear the testimonies that will come from your obedience to God!" Did you hear that? It's your obedience to God. Just the day before, on our ride to camp, I had been sharing about how the Lord was dealing with me about obedience.

I am not sure if a religious spirit may have been riled up reading that Mellony and I met in Vegas. On her text, she identified herself as Mellony that you met in Vegas. I already knew that, I had put her in my contacts as Mellony met in Vegas. Here is the exciting thing: she and I had met at the water show outside of The Bellagio. We got to talking and shared how we were both Christians. I told her that my husband and I love to come to Vegas and be stretched. Here, they spare nothing on expense and creativity and aren't we serving the Creator of the Universe? Mellony and I exchanged numbers but never had any communication until this day, July 12, 2011. We had met almost 2 years earlier.

The word Mellony gave us was a NOW word for us. Once again, we waged warfare that land and property would be granted and given to us. Exactly nine days later, we were given 100 acres for camp land. We are now believing that the provision will come to build this camp, where truly no child will be left behind.

This is what I pray you get from this book, a passion to pray and to realize He works through people. His desire is to give us divine connections. There truly is no distance in the realm of the Spirit.

CHAPTER 21

Connecting the Dots

As children, we've all enjoyed connecting the dots in coloring books. Our Heavenly Father enjoys playing connect the people. These connections should not just be limited to your geographical location. Through prayer, I've picked up many thrilling and unique assignments. Even weather patterns have been interrupted to get me to the right places and people. My friend and prophet, Ed Traut, has said over me that I have experienced such protection as I have found myself in unusual places, meeting people God intended me to meet.

The story of how I met Ed and his wife was one of those unusual circumstances. Bryan and I had plans to go with friends snow skiing in February 1996. The night before we were to leave for West Virginia, the weather man said a strange heat wave had hit up north. There was no snow in this normally winter wonderland. I am not one who likes to be cold…was God favoring me? I told everyone who would be traveling with us to pack swimsuits and we would just head to sunny Florida instead. As I set out to make reservations, 3 1/2 hours had passed and I had not found one room available anywhere on the East Coast. I remembered a few weeks earlier someone had told me about a revival that was going on in Brownsville, Florida. I had this thought: I wonder if we are supposed to go? I called for availability and found room in a hotel on Pensacola Beach. Ok, so I did not hear an audible voice, but I knew God had shut doors for a purpose. No snow in February in West Virginia and no rooms available from Jacksonville to Ft. Lauderdale. Since there was an available room in Pensacola, we said, "Brownsville Revival, here we come."

Service had already started when we arrived. We enjoyed the praise and worship and then they announced we would have a short break. Well if I haven't made it clear to you the reader yet, I love people! I see every day as an opportunity to make a new friend.

God had plans for me this night to really connect the dots. Standing in front of me was a man and his beautiful wife. During the break time, he turned around and said, "I'm Milton and this is my wife Pat." Then he asked for our names. I could tell he had a personality like me and that every function gave him an opportunity to make new friends too! He also introduced me to Ed and Louisa Traut. Ed and his wife were from South Africa and they wanted to come and see what God was doing in Brownsville.

My husband was used to me talking to anyone who would talk back. He had gone during this break to check out the sound system. When he came back, I introduced him to all my new friends. The service resumed and Carter, who was 3, at the time needed to go to the bathroom. I took him out and my new friends were in the lobby. Milton told me if we were ever in Montgomery or Birmingham to give them a call and we could meet. I told him we would be in Birmingham the next month to see Kenneth Hagin. He gave me a business card and I went back into the service.

When we were riding back to our hotel after service, I pulled out the card. I noticed it said Greyhound Track. I asked those with us what a greyhound track was. One of the guys said, "Rhonda, remember you had a vision a few weeks ago of dogs running in a big circle in the dirt?" I said, "Yes I do!"

Please know that we don't live our lives being led by visions or prophetic words. We believe in Romans 8:14 that we are led by His Spirit. He does use visions and dreams and prophets to speak to us. Vision seeing was really new to me back then. We were having a prayer meeting and all of the sudden I saw the above vision with dogs running in a circle. It impacted me so much so that I shared it right then and there. I was hoping someone could make sense of why was I seeing this. At that time it made no sense to any of us. God wanted to connect some people and all we had to do was show up! We met Milton and Pat in Birmingham the next month and formed a special friendship that has continued to grow.

One time, they wanted us to come to Montgomery to pray for a family member. I remember lying in their guest bedroom that first night to go to sleep. I had a little religious spirit knock on my door. Bryan was already sound asleep and I woke him up. I said, "Bryan we can't stay here. They bought this house with gambling money." Bryan said, "We didn't drive so we have to stay." I tried to lay my head down and heard the voice of God speak loud and clear, "Rhonda what would you have done or said if you lived in the days of Hosea the prophet?" I said, "What do you mean Lord?" Then I heard so clearly, "He married a harlot. My ways are not your ways, go to sleep." I'm so thankful for that rebuke. I can't imagine our lives without Milton and Pat. Connections are God's business. He used them to get us in contact with Ed Traut who has been such a powerful ministry gift in our lives for so many years now. Of all the words Ed has released, there is one that excites me so much. He said about our church, "This is a praying church. Many people are not willing to touch man and God. In this church, you touch God with one hand and man with the other." What a thrill to touch people through prayer!

My husband was so excited about one of his God connections. I have told you about our drilling truck for Kenya. Bryan was doing research on which type truck would best suit our needs. He was put in touch with two Alabama men who owned a drilling rig similar to the one he was looking at. One thing led to another and Bryan, his brother Bob, and a friend Daniel Derrick, were on their way to meet these men. Mike McRae was a pastor and had been working with Mark Carpenter in preparation for he and his family to one day go to Africa to drill water wells. He and his wife were answering the call to go to the nations. Mike recently got great news from his denomination headquarters. Of all the places in Africa they could be sent, they were assigned to Nairobi, Kenya. Isn't God amazing to have connected us with someone with over four years of experience on the same type of truck we have now purchased? Mike was another one of those dots in the connection.

Prayerfully, at the time of publication, the truck will be in final preparation for shipment so that it can accomplish what it's been purchased to do.

CHAPTER 22

Hawaii Here We Come

Tuesday prayer is one of my favorite times. People come who are serious about His agenda. Many take their lunch break to come do business in prayer. Corporate prayer is powerful! In March 2011, during Tuesday prayer, we were praying and began to pray about the Pacific Ocean. As we were praying we covered that ocean and coast line much in prayer. Pastor Amy kept praying, "specifically the Pacific." I had a sense that Bryan and I were supposed to go to Bob Harrison's Increase Event in Hawaii. As we were praying that Tuesday about the weather and the Pacific Ocean, Pastor Eli told my husband, "I bet Rhonda doesn't realize she's covering Hawaii." I didn't! I did great in geography in school, but somehow Hawaii and the Pacific were not connecting for me this day.

Riding later that day to a hair appointment, one of my spiritual daughters called to tell me that she felt Bryan and I needed to go to the Hawaii Increase Event. She said as she heard me praying about the Pacific Ocean and she thought I should go. Then she heard me pray that if someone would obey with their time that God would release a blessing. Then she said, "I believe you and Pastor are to obey and go to Hawaii."

Some of you reading are probably thinking, "Why would anyone have to pray about going to Hawaii?" Being in the right place at the right time is AWESOME! You need to know, Bryan and I don't need another trip. It's imperative for us to be places that He needs us to be.

Each year in March, we host our 31 Woman conference. We were getting ready to go to prayer that Friday morning when someone from home sent us a text about the tsunami. We flipped on the TV and watched with amazement what had happened in the world. An earthquake and now a tsunami was threatening to damage Hawaii? Boldness rose up inside of us girls in that oceanfront room at Myrtle Beach. The weather man had the minutes counting down and was showing the coastline in Hawaii. We rose up with our authority in prayer and said, "Oh no you don't devil! That water is not coming to damage Hawaii!" We were fully persuaded that no damage would happen because He had us praying and covering His plans just two days earlier.

Bob Harrison's event took place with no interruptions. Bryan and I obeyed and made time to be where He needed us to be. These conferences are truly unlike any I have ever been to. Great details are put into creating an atmosphere and environment for increase in every arena.

A personal favorite speaker at this conference for my husband is Myles Monroe. The session had taken place and Bob had dismissed us for a small break before the next session started. Of course I had made some new friends and was excited to visit for a few minutes in the lobby. I came back in just before the next session was to start.

Bryan said to me, "I just got off the floor!" My thoughts were, did he trip? Surely a move of God did not just happen and I missed it. What happened? Bryan had shaken hands with Bob while he was giving his offering. Myles Monroe was standing there, turned to Bryan, laid hands on him and said, "I hear your church will touch 17 nations." The power of God and my husband had an encounter right then and there!

It would be several weeks later that I was praying with a group and felt an unction to look in my prayer journals. My unction was to look at February 2005. The girls I pray with are used to me saying to get the journals and see what we prayed about at such and such a time. God wanted to confirm to me the prophetic word Myles had spoken to Bryan. I was so surprised to see on February 2005, we had prayed about our church being in 17 places! Wow! Had we not kept a prayer journal, we would have never remembered that. Keeping a journal of what He speaks to you in prayer is one of the best habits you, as a House of Prayer, can develop.

CHAPTER 23

Walmart Wants Our Church

On December 7, 1998, we received a prophetic word from Pastor Tracy Harris. "How many churches do you think would like to have this property? They couldn't see it but you saw it because of the light of the knowledge. Yes and that's not all the Glory you will see if you'll continue to follow me. I'll take what you paid for this place and the debt I will erase and then I'll double the price of this property, and you will see that you go out in victory, financially."

At the time of this prophetic word we as a church were on Wylds Road. God allowed this pastor to see into our future as a church and prophesy this amazing story that I am sharing now.

My husband was contacted by a commercial real estate agent and was told that a company was interested in purchasing our facility. It would be quite a few months before we knew Walmart was serious about this purchase. Many hours of talks, and on our end prayer, took place before we said yes. We felt this was part of God's plan for our ministry. It was so exciting that Walmart wasn't interested in any of the contents of our building…but it gets better! They said we could have anything in the building, lights, doors, and even toilets! All they wanted was our land. At this writing, we have closed down the newest sanctuary. We have returned into the first sanctuary that we renovated on this property and moved into in June of 2005. Bryan and I think we pastor the world's greatest people. They have been so flexible and made our move such a smooth transition. Because this sanctuary is smaller, it meant more services. There has been more work on everyone and yet no one has complained.

We had thought with Walmart purchasing our current property that this would be the time we could finally build on the 32 acres on Lewiston Road. Whenever a huge corporation makes a move, it takes months and months for it to happen. Once they tell us everything has gone through, we only have four months to let them have this property.

This is hardly enough time to build a brand new facility. As soon as Walmart started pursuing us, my husband began meeting with architects. He would tell the church when he had meetings with planning and zoning. We made prayer a priority over ever decision and every meeting. Building on undeveloped property comes with another set of rules and lots of them! We have had much favor with the officials in the county that this property is in.

We felt in our hearts that the Walmart deal would go through, but wisdom says you wait until you have signed papers. Wisdom is the voice of God. My husband is such a man of prayer and he always endeavors to follow that voice.

It was obvious by now that God has another property for our church on our way to our Promised Land. But where is that property? After more prayer and searching, my husband found a building that will not just suit our needs but be perfect for us. We put a contract on this property and a few weeks later closed the deal with Walmart. This newest purchase can be ready in less than four months for our church to move into!

God has another blessing in store for us with our promised land property. The county and the state have agreed that we will not have to spend several hundred thousands of dollars on a special lane. They are going to be taking care of that.

In 1997 we were given one of our very first prophetic words as a ministry: "It is not the hour that I inhabit buildings made with hands, but it shall be that I shall specifically choose locations where My people have called out to me. I shall place My name there and they shall be known as Houses of Prayer."

To us, prayer is a privilege and such a high responsibility. Our success as individuals and ministry can only be credited to this one thing, prayer.

Gross darkness may be covering the earth and the people, as Isaiah said, but it is time for us to arise and shine for our Light has come. (Isaiah 60:1 NKJV) How do we do that? 2 Chronicles 7:14 (NKJV) says, "If My people who are called by My name will humble themselves, and PRAY and seek My face, and turn from their wicked ways, then will I hear from Heaven and will forgive their sin and heal their land."

I pray that you've been stirred and provoked. **Prayer Is a Holy Occupation!**

Made in the USA
Charleston, SC
20 September 2013